CORE LANGUAGE SKILLS

Prefixes and Suffixes

Kara Murray

PowerKids
press.

New York

Published in 2015 by The Rosen Publishing Group, Inc.
29 East 21st Street, New York, NY 10010

First Edition

Editor: Sarah Machajewski
Book Design: Jonathan J. D'Rozario

Photo Credits: Cover Tyler Olson/Shutterstock.com; p. 5 Monkey Business Images/Shutterstock.com; p. 10 SLP_London/Shutterstock.com; p. 11 lanych/Shutterstock.com; p. 13 benedektibor/Shutterstock.com; p. 15 Melissa King/Shutterstock.com; p. 17 Lena Lir/Shutterstock.com; p. 20 FloridaStock/Shutterstock.com; p. 21 Pressmaster/Shutterstock.com.

Library of Congress Cataloging-in-Publication Data

Murray, Kara.
Prefixes and suffixes / by Kara Murray.
p. cm. — (Core language skills)
Includes index.
ISBN 978-1-4777-7349-9 (pbk.)
ISBN 978-1-4777-7350-5 (6-pack)
ISBN 978-1-4777-7348-2 (library binding)
1. English language — Suffixes and prefixes — Juvenile literature. I. Murray, Kara. II. Title.
PE1175.M87 2015
428.1—d23

Manufactured in the United States of America

CPSIA Compliance Information: Batch #CW15PK: For Further Information contact Rosen Publishing, New York, New York at 1-800-237-9932

CONTENTS

WORD PUZZLES

    Did you know that adding a special beginning or ending to a word can change its meaning? We call them prefixes and suffixes. A prefix is a group of letters that goes in front of a **root word**. A suffix is a group of letters that goes at the end of a root word. Prefixes and suffixes change the root words they're added to.

    Think of root words, prefixes, and suffixes as a **puzzle**. Each piece of the puzzle has its own meaning. When you put the different meanings together, you make something entirely new.

Figure It Out

"Re-" is a prefix that means "again." Adding the prefix "re-" to the root word "do" makes the word "redo." What does this new word mean? Find the answer to this question and the others in this book on page 22.

Knowing how to use prefixes and suffixes will improve your reading, writing, and speaking skills.

MAKING OPPOSITES

Knowing prefixes can double the number of words you know. Some prefixes can be used to make a word that's the opposite of a root word. If you know a word *and* its opposite, you know two words instead of one.

Prefixes that make opposites mean "not." The most common are "un-," "dis-," "im-," and "non-." Let's use the word "happy" as an example. "Happy" is our root word. Adding the prefix "un-" to the word "happy" makes the new word "unhappy." We know the word "unhappy" means "not happy." See how easy it is?

Figure It Out

Look at the following prefix puzzles. Can you tell what the new words mean?

dis- + agree = disagree

im- + possible = impossible

non- + sense = nonsense

Chart of Words with Prefixes Meaning "Not"

prefix	+	root word	=	new word
dis-	+	able	=	disable
im-	+	polite	=	impolite
non-	+	fiction	=	nonfiction
un-	+	friendly	=	unfriendly

WHERE AND WHEN

Some prefixes give us a clue about *when* something happened. The prefix "pre-" means "before." If you must prepay for the camp you're going to this summer, you know you must pay before camp starts. The prefix "post-" means "after." If you get invited to a postgame party at your teammate's house, the party will be after the game.

Other prefixes tell you *where* something is found. The prefix "under-" means "below." If you read that a plant's roots grow underground, you know they're below the ground.

Figure It Out

Can you figure out what the red words mean? "Midway through our trip to the aquarium, I saw a beautiful underwater creature!"

Chart of Words with When or Where Prefixes

prefix	meaning	example
mid-	middle	midday
post-	after	postwar
pre-	before	predinner
under-	beneath	underarm

MORE PREFIXES

There are too many prefixes to list them all, but they all work in the same way. Remember, adding a prefix is like a puzzle. Think of the root word's meaning, and then apply the prefix to that.

If someone tells you this chocolate is semisweet, you can imagine how it will taste.

"Semi-" is a common prefix. It means "half." Let's say you wanted to show someone a half circle. You could describe it as a "semicircle." The prefix tells them you're talking about half of a circle. Can you use this thinking to figure out what "semisweet chocolate" means? It means "chocolate that's only half sweet!"

Figure It Out

"Mis-" is another common prefix. It means "wrongly." Add "mis-" to the root word "understood." What does "misunderstood" mean?

SEMICIRCLE

STUDYING SUFFIXES

Suffixes work the same way prefixes do, but they help us with different things. The suffixes "-s" and "-es" tell us when there's more than one of something. For example, one book is just a book. If you want to talk about a whole library, add "-s" to "book" to make "books." Now you know there's more than one.

Suffixes also help us **conjugate**, or change, **verbs**. We use "-s" for the present **tense**, or something that's happening now. We use "-ed" for the past tense, or something that happened in the past.

Figure It Out

Suppose you want to say how your brother got home from school yesterday. Would you say, "Jack **walks** home from school" or "Jack **walked** home from school"?

"Jack smiled when this picture was taken" is something you could say to describe Jack's face in this picture. The verb "smiled" tells us he did it in the past.

CHANGING PARTS OF SPEECH

Suffixes have a lot of power. They're so powerful that they can change parts of speech. Some suffixes turn verbs into **nouns**. One suffix that does this is "-ion." It means "the act of." Adding "-ion" to the verb "attract" gives you "attraction." This noun means "the act of being attracted."

The suffix "-ness" means "state of." It works the same way as "-ion," but it turns an **adjective** into a noun. Pairing the adjective "soft" with the suffix "-ness" gives you the noun "softness." It means "the state of being soft."

Figure It Out

Can you use a suffix to create a noun that means "the state of being "kind"?

This dog has soft fur. The softness feels good to touch. Can you see how adding a suffix changed the way we used the word "soft?"

15

MAKING VERBS

Suffixes can also change adjectives into verbs. That means you turn a describing word into an action word. You can use the suffix "-ize" to do this.

Take the adjective "equal." Adding "-ize" to it makes the verb "equalize." If you don't know what "equalize" means, use the adjective and suffix to help you. If you know "equal" means "the same," then you can figure out that "equalize" means "to make something the same."

You can also use "-ize" to turn nouns into verbs. The noun "magnet" becomes the verb "magnetize" by adding three simple letters.

Figure It Out

"Legal" is an adjective. When you add "-ize" to it, you change its part of speech. What part of speech is the word "legalize"?

This image shows the verb "magnetize" at work!

MAKING ADJECTIVES AND ADVERBS

Suffixes don't stop there! They can turn nouns into adjectives. The suffix "-ful" helps with this. It means "full of." If you add "-ful" to the noun "color," you make the adjective "colorful." Can you figure out what "colorful" means?

Nouns → Adjectives

root noun	+	suffix	=	adjective
accident	+	-al	=	accidental
joy	+	-ful	=	joyful
fool	+	-ish	=	foolish
power	+	-less	=	powerless
life	+	-like	=	lifelike

Some suffixes turn verbs into adjectives. One example is "-ive." "Create" is a verb. When you add "-ive," you make "creative," an adjective.

One part of speech is almost always recognized by its suffix—the **adverb**. An adverb most often describes a verb. Adding "-ly" to an adjective usually makes an adverb.

Figure It Out

Can you pick out the adverb in the following sentences? Look for the word that describes a verb. Hint: look for the word that ends in "-ly!" "It takes me a long time to make art. I draw slowly."

Verbs ⟶ Adjectives

root verb	+	suffix	=	adjective
enjoy	+	-able	=	enjoyable
differ	+	-ent	=	different
select	+	-ive	=	selective

19

There's one last thing to know about suffixes. They can change a word's meaning but still keep the same part of speech. The new word refers back to the old word. One example is "-ship." For example, "friend" and "friendship" are both nouns. A friend is someone you like, and a friendship is what you share with that person. The suffix "-hood" works the same way. You add "-hood" to "neighbor" to make "neighborhood," the place where your neighbors live.

Everyone who lives in these houses is part of the same neighborhood, or place where the neighbors live.

Prefixes and suffixes are great clues to help you unlock the meaning of new words. Try it in the next book you read!

Figure It Out

The words "member" and "membership" are both nouns, but only one of them has a suffix. If "member" means "someone who belongs to something," what does "membership" mean?

The friendship between these kids is very special.

21

FIGURE IT OUT ANSWERS

Page 4: "Redo" means "to do again."

Page 6: Disagree: "to not agree"; impossible: "not possible"; nonsense: "not making sense."

Page 8: Midway: "in the middle"; underwater: "below the water."

Page 11: Misunderstood: "understood wrongly."

Page 12: "Walked," because the "-ed" tells us it happened in the past.

Page 14: "Kindness" = "kind" + "-ness"

Page 16: A verb.

Page 19: "Slowly" is the adverb.

Page 21: "Membership" means "the state of belonging to something."

GLOSSARY

adjective (AA-jihk-tihv) A word that describes a noun.

adverb (AD-vuhrb) A word that describes a verb.

conjugate (KAHN-juh-gayt) To give the different forms of a verb.

noun (NOWN) A word that names a person, place, or thing.

puzzle (PUH-zuhl) A question or problem to solve.

root word (ROOT WUHRD) The simplest form of a word.

tense (TEHNS) A verb form that tells when the action happens.

verb (VUHRB) A word used to describe an action.

INDEX

WEBSITES

Due to the changing nature of Internet links, PowerKids Press has developed an online list of websites related to the subject of this book. This site is updated regularly. Please use this link to access the list: www.powerkidslinks.com/cis/pref